SCHIRMER PERFORMANCE EDITIONS

CZERNY
THE SCHOOL OF VELOCITY FOR THE PIANO
Opus 299, Books 1 and 2

Edited and Recorded by Matthew Edwards

On the cover:
Chez Moi, 1887 (oil on canvas),
Harriet Backer (1845–1932)
Private Collection / Photo © O. Vaering / The Bridgeman Art Library

G. SCHIRMER, Inc.

DISTRIBUTED BY
HAL•LEONARD® CORPORATION
7777 W. BLUEMOUND RD. P.O. BOX 13819 MILWAUKEE, WI 53213

Copyright © 2013 by G. Schirmer, Inc. (ASCAP) New York, NY
International Copyright Secured. All Rights Reserved.

Warning: Unauthorized reproduction of this publication is
prohibited by Federal law and subject to criminal prosecution.

www.schirmer.com
www.halleonard.com

CONTENTS

HISTORICAL NOTES
CARL CZERNY (1791–1857)

Although born into a rather humble family with few prospects of prosperity or good education, Carl Czerny is today a household name, well-known to pianists around the world. Through good fortune, and a degree of talent, he interacted with some of the most important names in both Classical and Romantic literature. The list of his contacts is nearly unbelievable: he studied with Beethoven and Clementi; taught Liszt, Thalberg, and Leschetizky; and associated with countless others including Chopin, Constanze Mozart (Mozart's wife), Franz Xaver Süssmayer (Mozart's pupil), Andreas Streicher (the piano manufacturer), and many more. He was the first—or at least one of the first—to perform many of Beethoven's works, and wrote original compositions of such popularity in his day, that publishers were willing to print anything he submitted. Very often, they did not even care to hear or see it before the contract was signed.

Without doubt, Czerny lived in interesting times, and was privileged to observe first-hand the transition from the Classicism of Haydn and Mozart to the passion of the Romantics. Of course, none other than Ludwig van Beethoven was his guide through this most significant progression. Czerny stood as an observer at the crossroads of these two styles, but he also saw—and, to a great degree, assisted in—the transformation of keyboard technique. By the combination of the fame of his publications, and his successful teaching career, he became one of the foremost authorities on piano playing during this time. Even today, his legacy is sustained by his multiple collections of exercises and pedagogical works. Though his life is primarily summarized by these, a thorough study would reveal a man of many skills and interests.

Czerny's grandfather had been a violinist, and his father, Wenzel Czerny (1750–1832), played several instruments, including piano, organ, and oboe. Wenzel did not marry until 1786, delayed by his fifteen years of service in the army.[1] Carl, who would be the couple's only child, was born in Vienna, Austria, on February 21, 1791. The family briefly moved to Poland, but returned to Vienna in 1795, where his father began a moderately successful career of piano teaching and piano maintenance.

It is no surprise, then, that Carl was attracted to the piano early on; his autobiography states that he began playing at the age of three, and by seven was also composing.[2] His parents kept him close to home, generally removed from most of his would-be playmates, providing ample opportunity for his musical interests. In addition, much of his education came from his father's piano students, who, as part of their lesson fees, tutored Carl in a variety of subjects including French, German, and literature. Yet about this relative isolation, he states that he "never missed the friendship of other boys, and never went out without my father."[3]

His father's skill as a pianist and teacher was at least good enough to give young Carl an excellent foundation in technique and sight-reading. He describes it thus:

> My father had no intention whatever of making a superficial virtuoso out of me; rather, he strove to develop my sight-reading ability through continuous study of new works and thus to develop my musicianship. When I was barely ten I was already able to play cleanly and fluently nearly everything by Mozart, Clementi, and the other piano composers of the time; owing to my excellent musical memory I mostly performed without the music. Whatever money my father could set aside from the scant pay for his lessons was spent on music for me…[4]

Perhaps the critical moment in the life of Carl Czerny was his introduction to Beethoven. One of Beethoven's closest friends was a man named Wenzel Krumpholz, who also happened to be a friend of the Czerny family. Through Krumpholz, Carl became aware of the great composer, and as soon as he was able, began playing as much of his music as he could find. Impressed by the 10-year old's pianism and musicality, Krumpholz agreed to take the boy and his father to Beethoven's home for a formal introduction.

The apartment was high above the street, and was rather unkempt and disheveled. Other musicians were there rehearsing, but they quickly became an impromptu audience for Carl as he sat down at Beethoven's piano to play. He performed the first movement of Mozart's C-major piano concerto (K. 503), and Beethoven's own recently released Pathétique Sonata. When he finished, Beethoven uttered the words that quite possibly set Czerny's future success in motion: "The boy is talented, I myself want to teach him, and I accept him as my pupil. Let him come several times a week."[5]

Although the lessons lasted little more than a year due to Beethoven's growing need to focus on composition and the Czernys' financial situation, the relationship continued to grow until Beethoven's death in 1827. Czerny often worked closely with him, even writing the piano reduction for the publication of *Fidelio*. He also taught piano to Beethoven's nephew Carl, and gave widely successful early performances of Beethoven's works.

Performing never took a central role in Czerny's career—in fact, he cancelled his very first concert tour in 1805 even though it was supported by Beethoven himself![6] Instead, he turned his attention to teaching and composing, and found significant success in both areas. For many years, he taught twelve hours daily, and, by means of his prominent reputation, was able to charge very well for the instruction. While it was common for him to teach many of the most talented young people of the day, at least one eclipsed them all. Czerny describes the first meeting like this:

One morning in 1819... a man brought a small boy about eight years of age to me and asked me to let that little fellow play for me. He was a pale, delicate-looking child and while playing swayed on the chair as if drunk so that I often thought he would fall to the floor. Moreover, his playing was completely irregular, careless, and confused, and he had so little knowledge of correct fingering that he threw his fingers over the keyboard in an altogether arbitrary fashion. Nevertheless, I was amazed by the talent with which Nature had equipped him.[7]

Rarely does one hear such a dismal description of the great Franz Liszt, but such was Czerny's first impression. Over the next fourteen months, he worked with the boy every evening, requiring him to learn rapidly and work tirelessly on technical exercises including Czerny's own works.[8]

If we combine Czerny's published and unpublished works, his compositions number more than 1,000. He wrote symphonies, variations, arrangements, chamber works, and sacred choral works in addition to his numerous pedagogical works. Not all of his music was received well—in particular, Schumann's review of a piano work entitled *The Four Seasons* stated that "it would be hard to discover a greater bankruptcy in imagination than Czerny has proved."[9] Harsh, to be sure, but many of the greatest pianists, including Liszt and Chopin, played his works throughout the continent, to great acclaim. To this day, many of the sonatas are regularly performed.

Professionally, Czerny's reputation remained generally high throughout his life. Personally, however, he remained alone, never marrying. His brief autobiography, which describes his life to 1842, ends rather abruptly with the following sentence: "In 1827 I lost my mother and five years later (1832) my father, and was thus left all alone, since I have no relatives whatever."

Carl Czerny died on July 15, 1857. A humble beginning, a quiet passing; but in between, a remarkable life.

– *Mathew Edwards*

PERFORMANCE NOTES

Practice is the great Magician, who not only makes apparent impossibilities performable, but even easy.

Industry and practice are the Creators and Architects of all that is great, good, and beautiful on the earth.

Genius and Talent are the raw materials; industry and practice are as the graver impelled by an expert hand, which from the rude block of marble, forms the beautiful statue. [10]

The School of Velocity for the Piano, Op. 299

The fifty-year period spanning from 1785–1835 could arguably be described as the greatest transformational era for the piano. A vast number of developments in the construction of the instrument brought significant change in its music and in its technical requirements. Needless to say, composers and keyboardists from all over Europe wrote works and instruction methods to accommodate and educate performers young and old. Some of the greatest contributors include Hummel, Clementi, Kalkbrenner, Moscheles, and so many others. In the middle of all of these, and in many ways rising above them all, are the works and methods of Carl Czerny.

Czerny's pedagogical work spans an extremely wide range of technical ability, from the simpler openings of the *Practical Method for Beginners*, Op. 599, to the virtuosic etudes of this book, and *The Art of Finger Dexterity*, Op. 740. Across his exceedingly large output, countless technical topics are covered in numerous iterations. Scales and arpeggios are pervasive, along with thirds and other double notes, octaves, trills, leaps, chords, exercises for right hand and left hand, repeated notes, legato playing, staccato playing, ornaments; the list is nearly endless. Although the occasional argument may be made that a few of his exercises are impractical, the vast majority of his writings can still be used to great effect, and when employed appropriately, can be very useful to any pianist.

Further, while these etudes and exercises were certainly written with an eye toward improving technique, it is also important to remember that they are not exclusively technical works, devoid of musical merit. Indeed, these and countless additional exercises were written to improve one's technique in preparation for the difficulties contained in other, more naturally musical works. It would seem obvious, then, to practice the exercises in as musical a manner as possible; the practice of searching for musical meaning in a simpler piece will have great benefits when learning a work of deeper musical importance.

Practicing this entire volume would certainly improve one's technique, but one should remember that Czerny often wrote specific exercises for certain pieces, or for passages within a piece. In fact, he stated that he sometimes paused in the middle of a piano lesson to dash off an exercise for the problem his student was experiencing at that moment. It would be wise, then, to practice etudes from this book that focus on difficulties contained in other works being studied.

Technique and Physical Approach

Overall, a defensible approach to piano technique is one of relaxed arms and hands, rounded fingers supporting the weight of the arm, and freedom and economy of motion. It is understandably difficult to convey the subtleties of piano technique in just a few words. At the very least, tension should be avoided, and careful attention should be paid to the physical study of *how* a passage is best and most naturally played.

As an example, many of the pieces in this publication focus on scales and arpeggios. It is typically a sign of a technical problem if there is an unexpected accent or rhythmic unevenness in a scale or arpeggio. It is most important, in order to overcome this problem, that the fingers and hand (and by extension, the entire body) stay relaxed; by tensing your muscles, everything becomes more difficult. Relaxed playing gives much more freedom to the movements of the hand and arm.

Proficiency in any discipline requires a great deal of repetition, and pianists certainly spend countless hours "drilling" technique. Yet the best

kind of practice is that which constantly questions;
is this the best hand position? Is there a smoother
fingering? How can I phrase this better? Not all
passages will "become correct" if they are simply
reiterated ad nauseam.

Pedal

Czerny himself recommended little pedal in
works written before Beethoven, but greater
use for Beethoven and following composers.[11] In
these works, pedal can be applied where necessary
for connecting lines and phrases, and in a few
other places where color or effect may be more
important than perfect clarity.

Tempo

The metronome markings found in the original
edition of this volume are extremely fast,
appropriately suited to the title "School of
Velocity." However, we must consider that the
instrument for which Czerny was writing was
significantly different than what we use today.
Overall, the touch was considerably lighter than
modern pianos, which allowed passages to be
played faster than may now be comfortable.

As a result, we chose to include in this edition
two sets of tempos at the beginning of each
work. The first tempo is Czerny's original, given,
at least, for the sake of historical accuracy. The
second is actually a suggested range of tempos,
serving as a more general goal, rather than a
specific requirement.

Fingering

Remember that the fingerings given here are
suggestions only. Every hand is different, so every
fingering should be examined; don't try to force a
fingering that may not work for you!

Generally, the following few principles apply to
fingering choices:

- A relaxed hand: In the majority of cases the fingers
are kept close together, and the hand moves as a
unit. This more easily allows the fingers to stay
relaxed and the hand to move both faster and
more smoothly. Of course, stretches are required
when extending to the octave and beyond, but
allow the hand to move toward the extended
note, keeping the fingers relaxed.

- Economy of motion: this applies to the fingers
alone, as well as to the entire hand. Minimize
the number of crossovers in a passage grouping
as many notes into one hand position as possible.
Imagine, for example, if a simple C-major
arpeggio over three octaves were played with
only the first and second fingers; there would
be several hand positions, creating a much more
difficult passage.

Notes on the Individual Exercises

No. 1: Presto

Czerny begins with descending and ascending
scales for the right hand. The sixteenth rest
should be absolutely precise or it will cause the
passagework to sound out of tempo, or uneven.
The music is found mainly in the harmony; so play
the left hand alone a number of times to focus
on the shape of the line. Then add in the right
hand, following along with the left-hand shape,
but filling in the "gaps" between the notes.

No. 2: Molto allegro

The attention is turned now to left-hand scales, but
with more musical content provided by the right.
Think of this piece as a conversation between the
two hands, perhaps even slightly contrapuntal.
Keep the hands relaxed while playing the parallel
scales in measures 13 and 14; listen carefully that
they are precisely together.

In measures 9–12, keep the thumb relaxed on the
top note of each scale; tension at the top will cause
the next scale to begin late, or be too accented.

No. 3: Presto

This etude can sparkle brilliantly if the notes are
played with great clarity. Don't grab the four
notes as one unit, but play intentionally from
bottom to top of each group. This requires a bit of
patience (at any tempo) in the last two sixteenths;
one may tend to rush these two in an effort to
begin the next set. The first note of each set of
sixteenths can lead the musical line of this work;
think "weight," not "accent."

No. 4: Presto

An etude for turns and for finger-crossing, use this exercise to focus on the heart of the difficulty: avoiding tension in fingers 2, 3, and 4. Rather than tightening the fingers together and forcing the turn to work, think of the three stepwise sixteenths as a (very) short passage. The hand then moves slightly with the passage rather than remaining in the same location, thereby clutching the notes. This is also effective in measure 9 where there are five descending stepwise notes. The fingering here includes a crossover; focus on keeping it as smooth as possible.

A good practice for the music of this piece is to play only the first note of each beat, along with the left hand, allowing the line to be understood a bit more without all of the sixteenth notes. This has to be modified slightly for measures 15–23, where the second sixteenth is the melodic note.

No. 5: Molto allegro

Scale technique returns in full force in this etude with equal attention given to both hands. The scales should be clean and even, enhancing the musical line of the opposite hand. Remember also that the first note of each scale may be important in defining the line itself.

One of the greater challenges in this piece comes from the parallel scales in measures 39–42. Specifically, navigating the varying distance between the last note of one scale, and the first note of the next can be difficult. For the left hand, the distance is consistently a ninth; in the right, it can be as large as a ninth, or as small as a fifth. For the larger intervals, do not anticipate the leap; this will result in rushing the last few notes of the scale, and a greater likelihood of missing the leap because of tension. Don't consider the leap until the scale is complete, then in one relaxed motion, move the hand rapidly to begin the next scale.

No. 6: Molto allegro

Clarity is critical in this work. For measures 1–7 and similar places, it is again important that fingers 2, 3, and 4 move independently of each other, not grasping together as a single group. If one is not careful, it may sound simply like a tremolo between the thumb and a chord cluster! Rather than focusing only on those three upper notes, concentrate on the interval between fingers 1 and 4, and allow the remaining notes to "fall" into place afterward. Other passages in the work are somewhat different, but still typically contain the three stepwise notes from this first example. In each case, focusing on the first note of the three will contribute to clearer playing.

No. 7: Molto allegro

This piece moves the exercise element of number 6 into the left hand. It should prove a very practical etude as it focuses on a common left-hand accompaniment pattern.

The caution of grasping the three stepwise notes applies here as well; see the comments to number 6 for suggestions. Of particular note is the left hand in measures 23–28. The thumb and finger 2 have a sort of trill motion in this passage, and it may be a struggle to keep a steady tempo. Keep the thumb relaxed and don't allow it to get too high over the keys; too much height will make the trill awkward and difficult.

No. 8: Molto allegro

In addition to a new element, this etude reviews a little bit of everything from the previous seven. Broken intervals are introduced—thirds in measure 1 and seconds in measure 39. For the thirds, try to employ a degree of rotation, similar to that used for tremolo octaves, but of obviously smaller scope. One way to practice this is to begin with an octave and gradually decrease the interval size down to the third. This should not be over-emphasized, as too much rotation will actually make the technique more difficult.

For the seconds, the main caution concerns the thumb; it is easy to release too much weight or force on the thumb, causing an unwanted accent, and possible an uneven pair of sixteenths.

No. 9: Molto allegro

The opening measure is not reflective of the overall difficulty of this etude! And yet, the measure does draw attention to an important exercise in playing all of these etudes smoothly and with minimal effort. Spend some time focused on just the five-finger pattern, working carefully to play each note clearly while keeping the hand and fingers relaxed. Allow the hand to move with the rise and fall of the notes and never tighten the fingers in an effort to play louder. As this book progresses, some of the etudes grow longer and somewhat more intense; endurance begins to become of greater importance. Learning to play the first measure in the manner described will go a long way toward relieving the tension and muscle tightness associated with an "endurance" etude.

No. 10: Molto allegro

While the Alberti bass figure may be the most obvious technical element of this work, Czerny also focuses on legato octave-playing, beginning in measure 11. Certainly the pedal can be used, but the octaves should be played with as much connection (physically and melodically) as possible.

For the left hand, be sure the rotation is as relaxed as possible. Don't "anchor" or hold the finger with the lowest note—typically fifth or fourth—as this will quickly become tiresome. Musically, the left hand is led by that low note; so, a slight emphasis is appropriate for creating the counterpart to the right-hand melody.

No. 11: Presto

Broken thirds are the main subject of this etude. A relaxed approach and slight rotation of the hand will help significantly with endurance. Also, be careful to keep the thumb light and not accented when it is at the end of the group of sixteenths.

There are more "melodic" notes here; the first of each pair of sixteenths could be considered part of the melody. Yet, always listen for the larger metric element, the dotted quarter pulse, so that the piece sounds as if it is in 4/4, rather than emphasizing each of the twelve eighth notes. This larger meter will help in making the work more musical and less digital. Voice the top left-hand notes for a counterpart to the right hand.

No. 12: Molto allegro

Heretofore, only arpeggios of one octave in scope have been presented. Now the arpeggios span two octaves or more, requiring careful study of the most difficult element of arpeggios—the crossover. When first attempted, most students will perform a crossover with a great deal of twisting in the wrist, and likely a flailing elbow! This is never the ideal approach, as it immediately limits the potential speed of the arpeggio. I believe this is in part a result of keeping the hand in position over the first four notes and then suddenly reaching for the new position (attempting a full octave move!) by pivoting over the thumb. Better, and ultimately easier, is to keep the hand moving—

slightly—through the first four notes, so that the crossing finger is closer to its note. Using a left-hand ascending arpeggio as an example, the hand/finger appears to pass directly over the thumb, rather than pivot on it. As always, the fingers and hand should be relaxed, in particular, the finger/thumb immediately preceding the crossover.

For the larger stretches in measures 13–17, be patient before the leap; don't anticipate it, and thereby lose notes before the leap. Practice the motion required between the two notes involved—keep the hand open, but not stretched, and move the hand/arm freely.

No. 13: Presto

This etude, while an excellent study in tremolo, should be rehearsed with caution, and a careful eye toward a good physical approach. A tremolo is essentially a rapid shifting or alternation of the weight of the hand from one finger to another. Most typically, these occur as octaves or sixths, but can appear in any size interval—even a trill can be approached as a very small type of tremolo. There are several important elements. First, the fingers involved should move with the rotation of the hand, and not independently. Adding an independent finger motion to the hand movement will tend to make an uneven and unsteady sound. Second, keep the rotation minimal. Rotating too far, or putting too much weight to one side only increases the amount of work needed to return to the other note.

Listen carefully to the rhythm of this work. With the sixteenths divided, it may be easy to insert pauses between the hands. Throughout the piece, anticipate the beats in both hands and listen very carefully to keep the three right-hand sixteenths exactly even, not rushed.

In the left hand, be sure to use the suggested fingering, or a good alternate fingering. This will help to create a melodic line rather than just a series of staccato eighth notes.

No. 14: Molto vivo e velocissimo

There are (at least) two fingering options for the primary technical study in this work. This concerns the finger choice for the second thirty-second note on beats 1 and 2. Placing the thumb on this note turns the work into a sort of finger-crossing etude; placing a 2 on it causes the emphasis to be on the rapid movement from the first note to the second. Either situation could be encountered in piano playing; my personal preference here is to use finger 2 on the note in question.

In measures 19–22 don't "grasp" the intervals, but rather play with the hand balanced over the center of them, as if they were a single note.

No. 15: Presto

At first glance, this appears to be little more than practicing chromatic scales, but this etude also focuses on quick repeated notes, as well as finger crossing (in very tight spaces!), and quick changes of position.

For the repeated note, be sure not to land too heavily on the first one; playing deeply into it will make the second far more difficult. The first note should be played with the finger almost moving upward. If the hand is already beginning to move toward the second note, this lift will occur almost naturally.

No. 16: Presto

While the fingering suggestions may seem excessive at first glance, they are necessary for navigating this fairly difficult etude; where two options are given, try them both to see which works best for you.

In places such as measures 12 and 13, where the thumb and second finger are involved, make sure the thumb is always close to the keys, and to the second finger. Don't allow the thumb to fall away from the hand or even behind the keys when it is not playing. Doing so will make the triplet figures uneven and abrupt.

No. 17: Molto allegro

Although the etude appears to have a single technical focus, there are several elements to be studied in this piece. The primary difficulty could be described as independence of the fingers, as the upper finger remains in place while the lower navigate sixteenth passages. First, be sure to play the first notes of each beat with a hand balanced evenly over both notes; don't favor one side over the other. Then, remembering that it takes more weight to press a key down than it does to keep it down, be sure to "release" some of that initiating weight as soon as the quarter is played. By keeping the quarter note down with as little "pressure" as possible, the remaining sixteenths can be played more freely. If the upper finger holds on tightly to

the quarter, the sixteenths will suffer as a result. This figure is reversed in measures 9–12 but the same principles apply.

The melody can be quite clear when voiced well over the sixteenths. Be sure to give it shape, and don't allow the last sixteenth of each beat to be accented.

No. 18: Molto allegro

The broken thirds and seconds have moved into the left hand for this comparatively difficult etude. As in number 16, a great deal of effort must be given toward workable and consistent fingering; patience is required. Keep rotation in mind throughout, even with the smaller intervals. In particular, avoid tightness in the thumb. This will also help keep the left hand below the right hand dynamically. Don't think of the right hand as accompanimental chords, but as the melody, with the top note voiced clearly.

No. 19: Presto

The general issue here consists of larger crossovers, as large as a fifth. As described in number 12, there may be a natural—but incorrect—inclination to twist the wrist in an effort to get the finger into position. As with arpeggios, keep the fingers relaxed and the hand in motion, moving over the thumb without pivoting.

The added difficulty here—and the distinction from number 12—is that the crossover is often immediately followed by a change of direction. Don't go too deeply into the crossover note, as if you were continuing downward, but imagine that the change of direction actually begins somewhere between the thumb and the crossed finger.

Look for melodic notes within the sixteenths to lead and shape the line.

No. 20: Molto vivace

Though difficult, this may be one of the more enjoyable etudes of the set. Without question, good relaxed rotation is the key element here. Fingers must be free of tension when playing and when not playing. Rotate freely over a central position within the interval.

Almost equal to the focus necessary for the technique is that needed for the music. This can be a beautiful and exciting etude by careful shading and voicing.

Final Thoughts

I have known of these etudes since the age of 10, and they appeared to my young mind as the pinnacle of piano technique. With a sense of fear and awe, I dutifully checked the lofty tempo markings assigned so long ago by Czerny, the master teacher and founder of the "School of Velocity," so that I could know the very definition of success, and begin my struggle to achieve it. Some of the tempos were slightly more attainable; for others, I could only conclude—with a degree of resignation—that I had not, and might not ever achieve the minimum requirements of virtuosity. Constantly, in my head, I heard the chanting, "Faster, faster!"

One of the benefits of aging is the development of perspective, which allows us to see things differently. I now understand the facts about Czerny's piano and how it differed from mine in countless ways. I also understand that while speed can be good, it is nothing without clarity; how impressive is a fast tempo when it sounds like mumbling? I see now that as a young pianist, I missed so many pedagogical elements of these etudes, blinded by my incessant metronome-chasing.

When practicing these etudes, please keep in mind every aspect of technique: speed, articulation, fingering, voicing, musicality, pedaling, phrasing, etc. Surely Czerny would have expected his own students to gain more from this volume than the achievement of a particular metronome marking.

And in the end, perhaps Czerny himself said it best:

> Whoever possesses the art of always producing from the piano forte a beautiful, harmonious, and smooth tone…and further who combines the highest degree of volubility with perfect distinctness and clearness, will execute even the most startling assemblage of notes, so that they shall appear beautiful, even to persons unacquainted with music, and give them unfeigned delight.[12]

Notes:

[1] Little is known about his mother—she is described by Czerny simply as "a Moravian girl."

[2] Czerny, Carl. "Recollections from My Life." Trans. Ernest Sanders. *The Musical Quarterly*, Vol. 42, No. 3. (Jul., 1956), p. 303.

[3] ibid., 305.

[4] ibid., 303.

[5] ibid., 307.

[6] Stephan D. Lindeman and George Barth, "Czerny, Carl," *Grove Music Online*, ed. Laura Macy: www.grovemusic.com (accessed 1 Feb. 2011).

[7] Czerny, Carl. "Recollections from My Life." Trans. Ernest Sanders. *The Musical Quarterly*, Vol. 42, No. 3. (Jul., 1956), pp. 314–315.

[8] Alan Walker, et al, "Liszt, Franz." *Grove Music Online*, ed. Laura Macy: www.grovemusic.com (accessed 1 Feb. 2011).

[9] Stephan D. Lindeman and George Barth, "Czerny, Carl," *Grove Music Online*, ed. Laura Macy: www.grovemusic.com (accessed 1 Feb. 2011).

[10] Gerig, Reginald. *Famous Pianists and Their Technique.* (Indiana University Press: Bloomington, 2007), p. 108–109.

[11] Ibid., p. 115.

[12] Ibid., p. 115.

The School of Velocity
for the Piano

Book 1

Carl Czerny
Op. 299

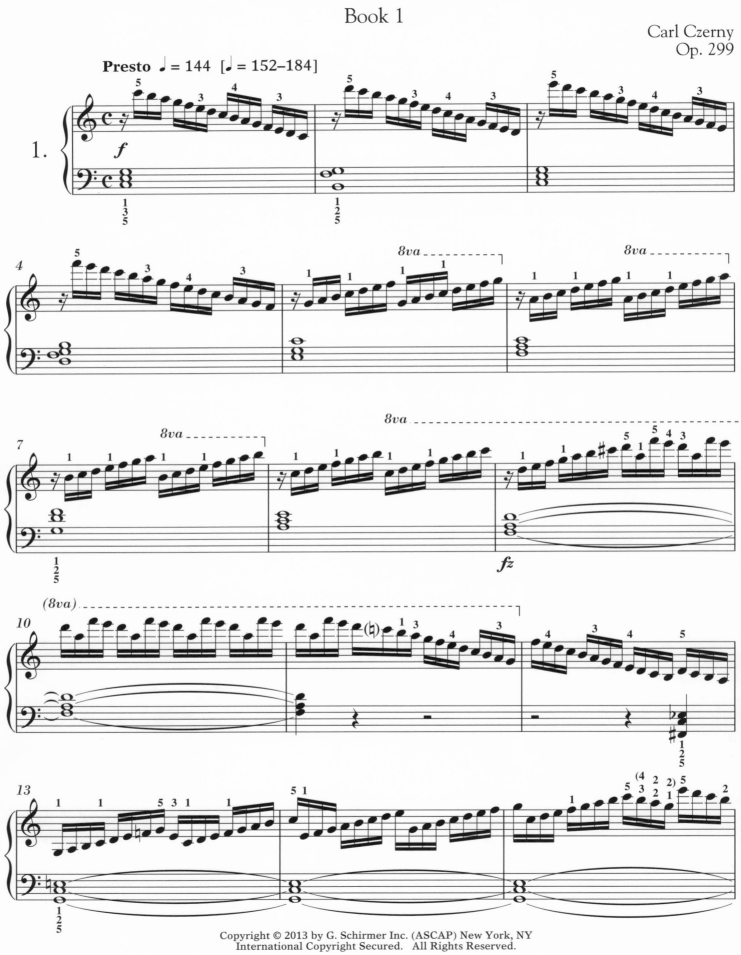

14

Book 2

Molto allegro ♩ = 144 [♩ = 120–152]

12.

44

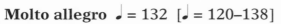

Molto allegro ♩ = 132 [♩ = 120–138]

17.

60

ABOUT THE EDITOR

MATTHEW EDWARDS

Matthew Edwards is a musician of many facets. As a pianist, he has been hailed by critics for his "...considerable talent...honest musicianship and a formidable technique." He has appeared throughout the United States, Asia, and Europe as recitalist, lecturer, guest artist, concerto soloist, and collaborative artist.

His competition winnings include the Grand Prize in the Stravinsky Awards International Competition, and First Prize in the Music Teachers National Association National Collegiate Finals. He received his Doctor of Musical Arts degree from the Peabody Conservatory in Baltimore, Maryland, where he studied with Robert McDonald.
Currently, he is Professor of Music and Director of Keyboard Studies at Missouri Western State University. His piano students there have won numerous prizes in major regional and national competitions. He has previously served as part of the faculty at several colleges, including the Peabody Conservatory of Music in Baltimore, and

Anne Arundel Community College in Maryland. As a lecturer, Edwards has been featured at the National Conference of the Music Teachers National Association, the World Piano Pedagogy Conference, and at the World Piano Conference in Novi Sad, Serbia. As a conductor and coach, he served as the rehearsal pianist/coach for the Annapolis Opera and musical director for Opera AACC. In 2012, he was guest conductor with the Jefferson City Symphony Orchestra. As a composer, he has had major works premiered in Chicago, Salt Lake City, and Baltimore, and he is a contributing author for the Hal Leonard Piano Library.

Edwards is a member of the Music Teachers National Association, and served a term on the Editorial Committee of American Music Teacher Magazine. He lives in Kansas City, Missouri with his wife, Kelly, and their three children, Audrey, Jackson, and Cole.